Ducklings

DISCOVER

Thanks for checking out the DISCOVER Books Series. Please note: All Rights Reserved. No part of this publication may be reproduced in any form or by any means, including scanning, photocopying, or otherwise without prior written permission of the copyright holder. Copyright © 2014

Ducklings

Ducklings are waterfowl and are the young of adult ducks. They belong to the family of, Anatidae. There are around 120 different species of ducklings. Many famous ducks have made us laugh over the years. Donald Duck is probably the most famous of them all. Some Ducklings live on farms. Others live in the wild. Let's explore the world of the Duckling. We will discover more cool facts and interesting things about this cute little bird.

Where in the World?

Did you know Ducklings can be found all over the world? The only place Ducklings can not be found is in the Antarctic. It is much too cold for Ducklings to survive there. However, some adult ducks do live on the Island of Auckland. This is part of the sub-Antarctic.

The Ducklings Home

Did you know Ducklings can live in fresh or saltwater? Ducklings and their parents need to live by a water source. This could be a lake, a river or even a pond. Some adult ducks will migrate from place to place. This means they wait until their Ducklings are adults, then they move to a warmer climate. They do this during the winter months.

The Body of a Duckling

Did you know most Ducklings are born very small? These little ducks have very short and stubby bodies. Their legs are long and thin. They have hard bill sthat helps them break through their eggs. The eyes of the Duckling are small and dark. They have one eye on each side of their head.

The Ducklings Feet

Did you know the Ducklings feet are webbed? Soon after a Duckling hatches from its egg, it can walk. Once they can walk, they leave the nest with their mother. They already know how to swim. Their webbed feet help propel them through the water. It's like when we wear flippers.

The Ducklings Feathers

Did you know Ducklings do not have "real" feathers? When Ducklings hatch, they are covered in a fuzzy down. This can be in many colors. Some are even bright yellow. After about 8 weeks, the Duckling will begin to sprout feathers. Soon after this, they will be able to fly.

What a Duckling Eats

Did you know Ducklings need lots of protein to grow? Little ducks will eat mostly meat. This includes; worms, insect larvae, snails and small fish. As they get older, they eat a lot of different foods like; plants, berries, frogs, salamanders, seeds and grain. Ducklings and their parents spend a lot of time looking for food.

The Duckling as Prey

Did you know the Duckling has lots of predators? Since Ducklings are small, many animals will prey on them. Large birds will snatch Ducklings. Animals like foxes, coyotes and cats will dine of Ducklings. Also animals like the raccoon and some snakes will eat the eggs of a duck.

Duckling Talk

Did you know Ducklings can make sounds? Before Ducklings grow up, they make a squeaking, peeping sound. They won't find their "quack" until they are much older. Some Ducklings, like the Muscovy, never quack. This species only hisses. Ducklings will squeak and peep when they are following their mom or having fun.

Duckling Eggs

Did you know Ducklings are born in a nest? Ducks build their nests on the ground. This is usually very near a water source. When the parent's construct the nest, it is made from twigs and mud. The mother duck will line it with her own feathers. This is to keep the eggs safe and warm.

Duckling's Mom

Did you know a Duckling's mom is called a "hen?" Depending on the species, a hen can lay anywhere from 7 to 16 eggs. She will protect her eggs by sitting on them. After the eggs hatch, the hen will lead her Ducklings to the water. This is to protect them from predators.

Life of a Duckling

Did you know Ducklings grow very quickly? Ducklings become full grown ducks at around 4 months-of-age. A healthy duck can live to be around 20 years-old. However, Ducklings have to stay very safe so they can reach adulthood. They do this by staying in the water and hiding in the tall reeds.

Crested Ducklings

Did you know the Crested Duckling has a big mound of feathers on its head? As they grow, this tuft of feathers will get larger. There can be up to 13 eggs in one Crested Duck's nest. The Ducklings will hatch out after 28 days. This breed of duck can be found in zoos around the world.

Indian Runner Ducklings

Did you know the Indian Runner Ducklings are not cared for by their mom? The mother Indian Runner duck will lay her eggs as she is running. If the eggs are not picked up they will get crushed. The Indian Runner Ducklings are born fuzzy and will never fly. They also do not waddle. They run.

The Muscovy Duckling

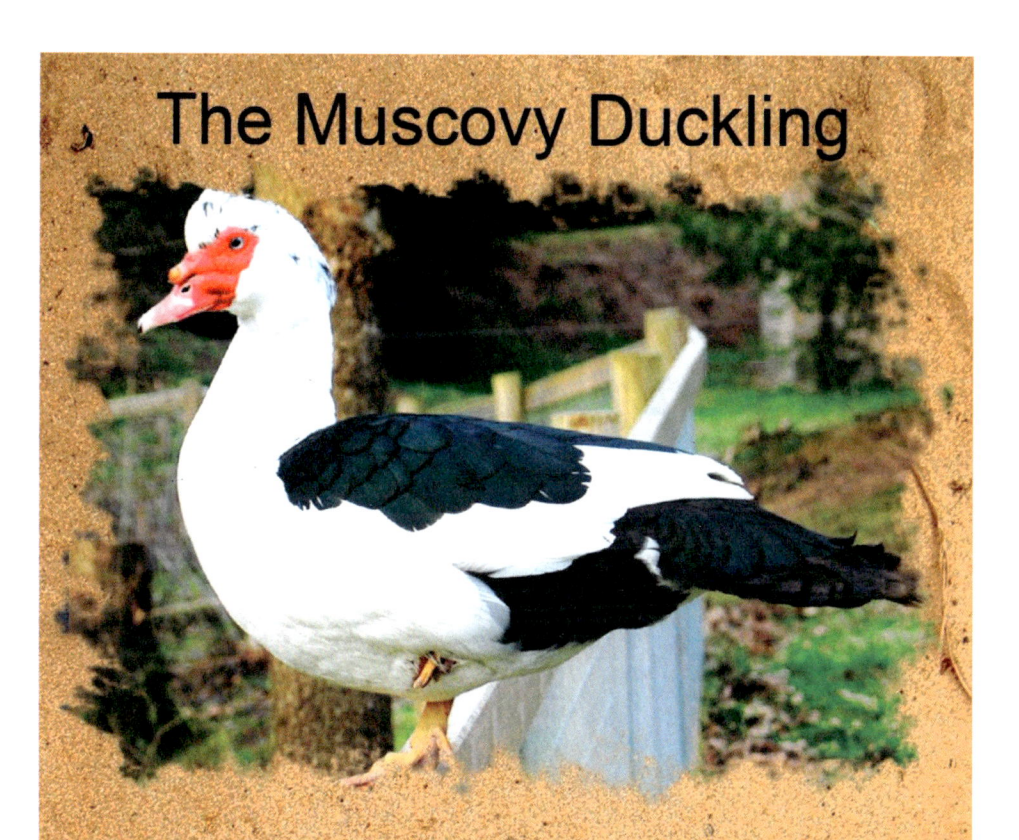

Did you know the Muscovy Duckling is born yellow and fuzzy? These Ducklings will break free from their eggs after 35 days. As the grow, their color will change from yellow to dark brown. They stay with their mom from 10 to 12 weeks. During this time they will grow in their adult feathers

Quiz

Question 1: Where is the only place Ducklings are NOT found?

Answer 1: The Antarctic

Question 2: What are Ducklings covered in?

Answer 2: A fuzzy down

Question 3: What types of water can Ducklings live on?

Answer 3: Fresh and salt water

Question 4: What sounds do Ducklings make?

Answer 4: Squeaks and peeps

Question 5: What is the Crested Duckling born with?

Answer 5: A big mound of feathers on top of its head

Thank you for checking out another title from DISCOVER Books! Make sure to check out Amazon.com for many other great books.

Made in the USA
Columbia, SC
26 March 2019